PROFESSIONAL ATHLETE

By Gayle Bryan

Checkmark Books®

An imprint of Infobase Publishing

Virtual Apprentice: Professional Athlete

Checkmark Books
An imprint of Infobase Publishing
132 West 31st Street
New York, NY 10001

ISBN: 978-0-8160-7896-7

The Library of Congress has cataloged the hardcover edition as follows:

Library of Congress Cataloging-in-Publication Data

Bryan, Gayle.
  Virtual apprentice. Professional athlete / Gayle Bryan.
    p. cm.
  Includes bibliographical references and index.
  ISBN-13: 978-0-8160-6759-6
  ISBN-10: 0-8160-6759-7
  1. Sports–Vocational guidance–Juvenile literature. 2. Professional athletes–
Juvenile literature. I. Title. II. Title: Professional athlete.
  GV734.3.B79 2007
  796.071–dc22

                2007005120

Checkmark Books are available at special discounts when purchased in bulk quantities for businesses, associations, institutions, or sales promotions. Please call our Special Sales Department in New York at (212) 967-8800 or (800) 322-8755.

You can find Ferguson on the World Wide Web at http://www.fergpubco.com

Produced by Bright Futures Press (http://www.brightfuturespress.com)
Series created by Diane Lindsey Reeves
Interior design by Tom Carling, carlingdesign.com
Cover design by Salvatore Luongo

Photo List: Table of Contents Adam Kazmierski; Page 5 Michael Flippo; Page 7 ACME/Bettmann/Corbis; Page 11 Minnesota Historical Society/Corbis; Page 12 Gayle Bryan; Page 14 Adam36/Dreamstime.com; Page 17 Randy Faris/Corbis; Page 20 Nice One Productions/Corbis; Page 22 Adam Kazmierski; Page 25 Philippe Lissac/Godong/Corbis; Page 27 Andrew Gombert/epa/Corbis; Page 30 Sarun Laowong; Page 33 Alan Crosthwaite/Dreamstime.com; Page 36 James Boulette; Page 38 Viorika Prikhodko.

Printed in the United States of America

BANG BFP 10 9 8 7 6 5 4 3 2 1

This book printed on acid-free paper.

CONTENTS

Welcome to the Wide World of Sports

It's game seven of the World Series, two outs, and bottom of the ninth. Your team is down by two but there are runners at first and third. You stroll from the on-deck circle to the batter's box exuding confidence; you live for moments like these. You give the pitcher the eye as you take a few practice cuts and then step into the box. You're not fooled by any of the junk he tries to bait you with. Instead, you wait for the money pitch and as soon as you swing the bat you know it's gone. The crowd explodes! You take your time rounding the bases, savoring the moment. As you round third toward the arms of your jubilant teammates you feel something running down your chin. You lift a hand to check it out and realize it is drool as you wake up from this amazing dream rubbing your chin.

Is there a baseball player alive that hasn't dreamed of saving the day with a game-winning homerun? The details might vary a little depending on your sport. Instead of the home run, it could be the three pointer that wins it at the buzzer, the Hail Mary pass in the waning seconds of the Super Bowl or the penalty kick that makes you champion of the world.

Many athletes dream of being a pro someday and there are some that actually make that dream come true. How do they do it and what's it really like when you get there? What are your odds of making it someday? Read on to find out how to

• get a front row seat at some of professional sport's most important milestones

• tag along with a professional athlete who, by the way, looks a lot like you

• take a sneak peek at some of the amazing technologies that are changing the way athletes compete

• find out what it takes to become a star athlete

• meet the people who make professional sports happen

• see what real sports pros have to say when kids like you ask them what it's *really* like to be a professional athlete

And while you're at it, do a few reality checks, investigate some resources, and test your skill at some pop quizzes. Ready for more? Bring on the virtual professional-athlete-for-a-day experience and find out for yourself if you've got what it takes to become a professional athlete.

What's your pick for a sports career?

CHAPTER 1

Athletes Then and Now

FUN FACTOID

In 2006, tennis player Maria Sharapova was the highest-paid female athlete, earning over $20 million including endorsements.

Professional athletes earn a living by playing sports. Sounds fun, doesn't it? Who wouldn't want to *play* for a living? Sure beats working. While professional athletes are fortunate to spend their days doing something many of us would give our right arm to do, it is not without its challenges. For every glorious *Sportscenter* moment there is never-ending training, conditioning, and fitness, not to mention a lot of time spent away from family and friends.

And, the reality is that very few athletes get to live their dream. Less than five percent of high school athletes become college athletes and less than three percent of college athletes ever become professionals. Be realistic, but don't spend too long crunching those numbers. At this point, who's to say that you won't be one of the lucky few to make the cut? And besides, as you'll soon discover, there's more than one way to make sports the center of a winning future.

But even so, you have to admit that the whole professional sports scene is a little crazy when you think about it. Young men and women make extraordinary (even obscene) amounts of money for playing a game. How did this happen?

"You don't **suffer, kill** yourself, and take the **risks** I take just for **money.** **I love** bike racing."
—CYCLIST GREG LEMOND

Even champion golf players like Tiger Woods have to practice.

Off-Season Options

REALITY CHECK

You've just finished a brutally long season and are faced with three months off. What do you do?

A Kick back and relax, indulge in all the unhealthy foods you couldn't eat during the season, enjoy this well-deserved break, and then hit the gym hard two weeks before you have to report to training camp.

B Take a few days off but maintain a moderate training schedule throughout your break.

If you picked A, you may not have the discipline it takes to survive as a professional athlete. Keeping your body in top shape has got to be a priority for a professional athlete.

Professional athletes get paid because people are willing to buy tickets to see them play. Throughout history, sporting competitions have drawn large crowds of spectators.

Some of the earliest recorded sports fans gathered to watch the Olympic games in ancient Greece and gladiators fight to the death in Rome.

While the history of sports goes back a long way, the idea of paying athletes is a fairly new concept. Until late in the 19th century, it was generally agreed that money would corrupt sports and that athletes should play solely for the love of the game. Of course the people espousing those views were mostly rich people who had the free time and the money to pursue their sporting interests. Stiffs who worked for a living didn't have the time to train or compete at high levels.

As sporting events became more and more competitive, a bit of hypocrisy developed as the upper class continued to insist that athletes compete as amateurs, but actually paid them out of their back pockets. This practice was known as shamateurism and an early example comes from the United Kingdom's Football Association. They prohibited their players from being paid but it would not be uncommon for a half a crown (equivalent to one-eighth of a Britist pound) to magically appear in a player's boot (soccer cleat) after a match. These hush-hush payments became known as "boot money."

Fast forward to the United States in 1869. The Cincinnati Red Stockings crisscrossed the nation as the first professional baseball team. Shortstop George Wright drew the largest salary, a whopping $1,400 (compared to the $9.8 million the Cincinnati Red's highest paid player, Eric Melton, earned in 2006). The Red Stockings' revolutionary venture into professional athletics didn't prove profitable for its owners so they returned to amateur status after the 1870 season, but the National League of Baseball Clubs was formed in 1876 and professional baseball was here to stay. You probably know this league under its current name, the National League. To this day their champion meets the champion of the American League (which was founded in 1900) every year in an exciting event we know as the World Series.

William (Pudge) Heffelfinger became the first "professional" football player when he was paid $500 to play for the Allegheny Athletic Association (AAA) in a game against the Pittsburgh Athletic Club (PAC). The $500 proved to be a good investment for the AAA when Pudge ran back a PAC fumble for a touchdown to win the game.

Let the Games Begin

The National Football League (NFL) was born in 1922 after operating for a couple years as the American Professional Football Association. Baseball had already established itself as the national pastime and the NFL didn't catch on in a major way until the 1950s when it got a huge boost from the growing popularity of television.

The National Basketball Association (NBA) is the latecomer when you look at the "big three" of team sports in America. It was formed in 1949 with the merger of the National Basketball League and the Basketball Association of America. Like football, the NBA took a while to grab the nation's attention. Great rivalries between players like the Boston Celtics' Larry Bird and the Los Angeles Lakers' Magic Johnson and the arrival of Michael Jordan, arguably the greatest athlete ever, gave the NBA a huge boost in popularity in the 1980s and 1990s.

On the individual side of things, 10 professional golfers competed for the first U.S Open title in 1895. The Professional Golfers Association (PGA) was formed in 1916 and now claims to be the world's largest working sports organization. In 2006 the PGA boasted the world's best paid athlete with Tiger Woods bringing in a staggering $87 million per year, including endorsements (money he is paid by big companies like Nike to help sell their products).

Professional tennis has been around since the early 1900s but the sport's four major championships, Wimbledon, the U.S.

CHECK IT OUT

Rent *Baseball,* a film by Ken Burns that documents the complete history of the sport.

Open, the French Open, and the Australian Open were not open to professionals until the 1960s.

There is no way to conclude a look at professional sports without mentioning the National Association for Stock Car Auto Racing, otherwise known as NASCAR. The first NASCAR race was held in Daytona Beach in 1948. NASCAR exploded in the 1990s and became a cultural phenomenon. Millions of fans from all walks of life buy tickets to NASCAR events every year and their television ratings rival those of major sporting events like MLB and NBA playoff games.

Girls Got Game, Too

Some of you girls may be thinking, that's interesting, but where do we fit in? With the exception of the All-American Girl's Professional Baseball League, which began in 1943 and ended in 1954, most of women's early forays into the world of professional sports were in individual rather than team sports.

The Ladies Professional Golf Association (LPGA) is the longest-running professional women's sports organization. It started in 1950 with 14 events and $50,000 in prize money and in 2005 featured 34 events that paid out $45 million.

Professional women's tennis took off in the early 1970s when Billie Jean King and eight other players signed contracts with publisher Gladys Heldman to play on a women's only tour. They were each paid $1 to legalize the contracts for a tour that didn't have a sponsor yet. The Virginia Slims Tour was born in Houston and paid out $309,100 in prize money its first year. In 2006 the number one player, Justine Henin-Hardenne, alone earned over $4 million in prize money.

Team sports have taken longer to get off the ground. The WNBA celebrated its 10th anniversary in 2006 and has enjoyed a longevity envied by other women's sports, but its players earn far less than their NBA counterparts. The maximum salary paid to a WNBA player in 2005 was $89,000 compared with the $15.3 million paid to the highest-paid NBA player. The difference is monumental but the women's league is young and still finding its audience. To its credit, the women's league managed to average 10,000 fans per game in only two years. It took the NBA 30 years to accomplish that.

CHECK IT OUT

Rent *A League of Their Own,* a movie telling the story of the All-American Girl's Professional Baseball League, starring Tom Hanks and Geena Davis.

Jackie Robinson, one of professional baseball's first black players, slides into home base.

Women's professional soccer burst onto the scene in 2000 after the U.S. women wowed the world with their historic victory over China in the 1999 World Cup in front of over 90,000 fans at the Rose Bowl. Their success was short lived and the Women's United Soccer Association (WUSA) folded in 2003. A small group of women earn a living as professionals by representing the United States on the Women's National Team in international events like the Olympics and the World Cup. Plans are underway to relaunch a women's professional soccer league in 2009. In the meantime, women who dream of playing soccer for a living play in leagues in Europe or Asia, or work for a living and keep their skills sharp by playing in amateur leagues like the WPSL and the W-League.

Professional women's soccer is making a comeback in the United States thanks, in part, to the efforts of players like Lindsay Tarpley.

There are currently two professional women's football leagues in the United States, the Women's Professional Football League (WPFL) and the National Women's Football Association (NWFA), but no woman is claiming to make a living playing football...yet.

Similarly, the National Pro Fastpitch (NPF) women's softball league is currently paying its players a small salary for a three-month season and hopes to be able to pay players year round as interest in their league grows.

This means that many female team athletes must find another means to support themselves in order to play. Women have come a long way, baby, but they still have a ways to go. Who's to say what kinds of new opportunities await the young girls just learning how to play a favorite sport!

Show Me the Money

How athletes get paid depends on what kind of sport they play. Team sport athletes like baseball or football players are under contract to a team and earn a salary, which might include a signing bonus and other bonuses based on how well the team performs. Athletes that compete in individual sports like golf and tennis are paid exclusively based on their performance. They enter tournaments and receive prize money based on how well they play. They are responsible for their own travel and expenses so, if things aren't going so hot, they can actually lose money. And, for every Tiger Woods or Roger Federer raking in the dough there are lots of pros wondering where their next meal is coming from and how they're going to get to the next tournament.

In addition to salaries or prize money athletes receive for actually playing their games, they can also make money from endorsements. Companies like adidas and Nike pay athletes for wearing their shoes and appearing in commercials to help sell them. Athletes also get hired by companies to make public appearances and to speak at meetings and events.

Television ushered in the era of big money in sports. Sporting events went from being local affairs that made most of their money from ticket sales to events that could be seen in households across the nation. Television networks pay big bucks to leagues and event promoters for broadcasting rights to sporting events. They in turn charge advertisers big bucks to show their commercials during sporting events. Just in case you are wondering what qualifies as "big bucks," networks paid $3.1 billion for the rights to broadcast NFL games in 2006 and advertisers shelled out $2.25 million to run a 30-second commercial during the Super Bowl.

Today's top professional athletes make outrageous sums of money. The really big sports stars have celebrity status equal to that of some of Hollywood's biggest stars. The very best like Shaq, LeBron, Mia, and Venus are on a first name basis with the public. Being a public figure has its perks, but it's not without a downside. Being recognized whenever you're out in public might be cool at first, but it gets old in a hurry. Having sordid details of your private life, whether real or imagined, become tabloid headlines or talk show chatter isn't a barrel of laughs either.

Of course, not every athlete makes Tiger Woods-type money. According to the U.S. Bureau of Labor Statistics, in 2004 the median income of a professional athlete was $48,310. That means half made more and half made less. So for every A-Rod out there making millions there are many more barely eking out a living or working a second job just because they love to play.

In this career, perhaps more than any other, it is important not to put all your

FUN FACTOID

Pay Day

The highest-paid athletes in 2006 were

➤ Tiger Woods - $87 million

➤ Michael Schumacher - $60 million

➤ Oscar De La Hoya - $38 million

➤ Michael Vick - $37.5 million

➤ Shaquille O'Neal - $33.4 million

➤ Michael Jordan - $33 million
(Pretty amazing since he retired in 2003)

➤ David Beckham - $32.5 million

➤ Kobe Bryant - $28.8 million

➤ Lance Armstrong - $28 million

➤ Valentino Rossi - $28 million

For millions of sports fans the day isn't complete without a look at the latest scores.

eggs in one basket. Even the most gifted athletes have a backup plan. You may be the most talented athlete on the planet, but your career can be over in an instant if you get injured.

Even the lifespan of a healthy athlete's career is much shorter than in more traditional jobs. Many athletes move on to second careers when their playing days are done. Former pros often show up in the broadcast booth or on the sideline as coaches. Others run successful businesses, sell cars, or become financial planners. It's important to think ahead about what happens when the ride is over.

If you decide, after much soul searching, that you've got the goods to pursue a career as a professional athlete, make the most of your educational opportunities. Don't waste the gift of a free education if you receive an athletic scholarship. Remember the statistic quoted earlier in the chapter; only three percent of college athletes ever make it to the pros. Even if you're good enough to be part of the three percent, you could suffer an injury that ends your career before it even begins and, the truth is, no one can play forever. So be smart. Play hard, but study hard too!

The Business of Sports

While you're thinking things over don't overlook the amazing realm of possiblities that exist in the sports industry as a whole. According to the *Sports Business Journal,* sports bring in a staggering $213 billion each year. That's twice as much as the U.S. auto industry and seven times more than the movie industry!

Take a look at where the *Sports Business Journal* says that some of the money comes from and you may find inspiration for a totally unexpected direction in your future sports career. Look at

- advertising on billboards, television, radio, and magazines

- sporting equipment and sportswear

- new facility construction

- licensed goods (like a T-shirt with your favorite team's logo on it)

- medical care for all those injured athletes

- sports-related magazines, computer and video games, videos and DVDs, and books

In every case, it takes lots of sports fans doing very specific, and in many cases very interesting, jobs to make pro sports happen. There are radio announcers to broadcast all the play-by-play action, advertising exectutives to create the cool ads we watch during the Super Bowl, architects to design sports arenas, journalists to write about the latest sports news, engineers to design sports equipment.

Honestly, there's bound to be something for anyone who wants to blend a love of sports with their skills and training. Get creative and who knows what you could end up doing!

But, if your heart is set on becoming a professional athlete, you know that fame and fortune is the upside. You've taken a realistic look at the downside, but the truth is you've got the fire burning in your belly. You must compete. Well, what are you waiting for? Lace up you shoes and let's get to work.

REALITY CHECK

Your Big Three

The official "big three" of U.S. sports are baseball, basketball, and football. But, just suppose you got to pick the top three sports to get the most television coverage, make the most money, and attract the best players. What three sports would you pick?

Athletes at Work

You are on the edge of your seat in the American Airlines Arena. The clock is ticking down and your beloved Miami Heat is down by two and the game is slipping away fast. The Heat has the ball and the inbound pass goes to Dwyane Wade. He lets it roll to almost half court before he picks it up. The clock starts running down from 10. He stutter-steps at the three-point circle and in the blink of a eye he has split two defenders, executed some crazy spin move, muscled his way to the basket, got fouled on the way up, and still managed to make the basket. He sinks the free throw and wins the game. You stay in your seat with your mouth hanging open. How does he do that?

You've seen the game winning heroics, but what you haven't seen is the constant training, practice, and sacrifices Wade has made to be able to perform at that level. Legendary Penn State football coach Joe Paterno says, "The will to win is important, but the will to prepare is vital." And Wade, like other outstanding athletes, has spent most of his life preparing to be the best.

For many of them, their worlds have revolved around their sport since they were kids. They've given up high school graduations, proms, and vacations with their family and friends to

> "They said **playing** basketball would **kill me. Well, not playing** basketball was killing me."
>
> —EARVIN "MAGIC" JOHNSON

take advantage of opportunities to be seen by scouts or play at a higher level. U.S. soccer star Heather O'Reilly explains, "I've just had to put soccer above everything else. I've always just thought of it as my biggest goal in life and that some things were

What's the game plan, Coach?

just going to have to be put on the back burner for the time being. That's consisted sometimes of missing vacations with family or spring break when my friends are all going somewhere fun. I've never just gone on a trip with my friends, ever. It's always been soccer related."

The sports superstar has constant pressure to perform. For every time our sports heroes deliver the magic moment there are more times when they don't. Michael Jordan, perhaps the best basketball player ever, put it in perspective when he said, "I have missed more than 9,000 shots in my career. I have lost almost 300 games. On 26 occasions I have been entrusted to take the game winning shot... and missed. And I have failed over and over and over again in my life. And that is why I succeed."

Contrary to popular opinion (especially among kids!), becoming a professional athlete is not for everyone. It takes enormous amounts of self-discipline and skill plus an ability to handle intense pressure, annoying fans, and the constant threat of physical injury. Of course, the payoffs can be equally enormous in terms of fame, fortune, and the joy of doing something you really love. But there are trade-offs and any aspiring athlete needs to face the facts and decide for him or herself if the pursuit of the game is worth it.

Or, as legendary football coach Vince Lombardi put it, "Football is like life, it requires perserverance, self-denial, hard work, sacrifice, dedication, and respect for authority." Of course, the same thing can be said of succeeding in any professional sport.

Are you cut out for that kind of success? Put yourself in a pro athlete's very large shoes and see for yourself what it's really like to play games for a living.

Just Another Day in the Life of a Sports Hero

You roll out of bed at 7:30 a.m. Since you had a game last night practice is a little later and you got to sleep in. You stumble into the kitchen and prepare a delicious soy protein shake to drink with your breakfast of a whole wheat bagel with peanut butter and a banana. After breakfast you lace up your running shoes and go for an easy three-mile run around the park just to get the juices flowing. You grab a quick shower and get dressed for practice.

Test Your Sports IQ

Match the pro athlete with their amazing feat of athletic prowess:

A Brandi Chastain

B Kobe Bryant

C Katie Smith

D Deion Sanders

E Wayne Gretzky

1 The only athlete that has played in both a Super Bowl and a World Series

2 Scored 92 goals in a single NHL season

3 Scored 81 points against the Toronto Raptors on January 22, 2006

4 The only player to win an ABL and WNBA basketball championship

5 Made the winning penalty kick in the 1999 Women's World Cup final

ANSWERS: A-5, B-3, C-4, D-1, E-2

You are just about to grab your keys when the doorbell rings. You open the door and find an official from the NBA. They're there for a random drug test. Fortunately, you are able to provide a specimen quickly so the inconvenience doesn't train wreck your whole morning. You understand the importance of keeping your sport clean, but it's hard not to be annoyed when someone randomly shows up at your door and asks you to pee in a cup.

You hop into your sports car and head over to the arena. Practice doesn't start until 10:00 a.m. but you've got to get there early to see the trainer. You sprained your ankle a few weeks ago when a player from the Bulls fouled you. The trainer wants to have a look and get you taped up for practice.

You head onto the court and start loosening up and shooting some baskets as the rest of your teammates straggle in. The mood is pretty light until the coach arrives. Warning: He's pretty ticked because he thinks your team got out-hustled in the game last night. Be prepared for an hour of brutal conditioning until he cools off.

After a short break to hydrate, you're back on the court running through some defensive drills. The coach is adding a new wrinkle to your zone defense, which he thinks will help you in your series against Detroit. It takes a while but you make the adjustment and feel ready to implement it into the game.

Practice winds down at about 12:30 p.m. and, even though the other guys start heading to the locker room, you stay out on the court. You've missed a couple key free throws late in games recently and want to work on them while you're good and tired. You put in an extra 20 minutes before making your way back to the locker room. The trainer has an ice bath waiting for you. It's not your favorite thing but you know it will be good for your ankle so you plunge in. When you've suffered enough, you towel off and head to the training table for your rubdown. Now that's more like it.

By now you are good and ready for lunch and catch up with some of the guys at a downtown deli where you know fans will leave you alone to enjoy a leisurely lunch. Afterward, instead

Spending extra time practicing may pay off in the game.

of heading home, you and the guys make your way back to the arena's state-of-the-art training facility for weight training. You run through the circuit your trainer has specifically developed for you and then you grab yet another quick shower and dress. The coach grabs you just as you head for the door. He wants to chat for a few minutes. It's nothing major. He just wants to see how things are going and make sure that you're on board with the new defense.

Getting Down to Sports Business

The second you jump back in your car, your cell phone rings. It's your agent. He is just calling to remind you that the photo shoot for the new line of tennis shoes you're representing starts in a half hour. He also tells you that *Sports Illustrated* wants to do a story on you and informs you that one of their writers will be following you around for a couple days next week.

He mentions a few other companies that want you to endorse their products and promises to have their proposals couriered over to your house. Endorsing products is a great way to get positive media exposure—not to mention a quick way to pick up some big bucks—so work with your agent to find the very best deals with the very best companies.

Finally, he asks if you remembered to call that crazy lady who's writing that book about pro athletes for middle school kids. You tell him you forgot but promise to do it as soon as you hang up. You spend the next 15 minutes answering questions about what it's really like to be a professional athlete before heading off to the photo studio.

It is now 3:00 p.m. and you are sitting in a chair while a makeup artist gets you ready for the shoot. You're glad that the guys aren't here to witness this humiliation but, then again, you

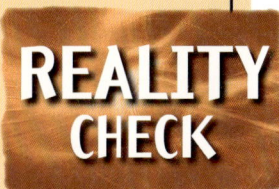

Can You Take the Heat?

You're in a nice restaurant having dinner with some friends when a group of fans interrupt your meal and ask for your autograph. Your initial response is to:

A Politely sign whatever they put in front of you because, after all, they're the reason you have a job.

B Tell the annoying bloodsuckers to bug off. Don't they know you have more important things to do than be harassed by a bunch of obnoxious fans?

If you picked B, you might need to work on your interpersonal skills before forging ahead on your quest to become a professional athlete. Without the fans, you're out of work, and if you make it big, dealing with them will become part of your everyday life.

What's a few thousand screaming fans when you are totally focused on your game?

have a cool shoe named after you, so who's complaining. The photographer is a pro and you know the ropes so you're done in less than two hours.

Night on the Town

You make it home at 5:30 p.m. wishing you had time for a nap, but you've got big plans for the evening. There's no game tonight so you've managed to squeeze in a dinner date with an old friend. You're enjoying some conversation while you're waiting for your meal at a nice restaurant when out of the corner of your eye you see the familiar sight of a small group of people whispering and looking in your direction. After a moment they decide it's really you and tentatively approach asking for autographs. You graciously oblige and sign everything, smiling and chatting up your fans. The only problem is the commotion has drawn even more attention and what was supposed to be a quiet evening out has turned into an autograph session. When you've finally signed the last autograph your food is there but it's cold and your friend is bored silly. You make a mental note to do dinner at home next time.

Before you head for home, you've got one more stop to make. One of your favorite charities is auctioning off a private training session with you as a fund-raiser. You put in an appearance to say hello and stir up some buzz about the top prize.

It's midnight before you get home and before you hit the sack you go over tomorrow's schedule in your head. You'll work out with the team in the morning before hopping on a charter flight to Detroit for another game. You'll have time to rest up in the hotel before heading to Auburn Hills.

Don't forget to call your accountant to set up a meeting to check on your investments. You wish you could just leave the financial stuff to her, but you've heard too many stories of pro athletes losing their shirts because they trusted their finances to someone else.

You probably should take a few minutes to get your stuff together but, hey, it's been a long day. It's time to catch some zzzzzs and get ready for another big day as a sports star.

Like baseball great Joe DiMaggio said about opening day, "You look forward to it like a birthday party when you're a kid. You think something wonderful is going to happen."

CHAPTER 3

Sports Tech and Trends

Today's professional athletes can run faster, jump higher, endure longer, and perform at a higher level than ever before thanks to advances in training techniques, better equipment and, unfortunately, in some cases performance-enhancing drugs.

Technology has impacted the progress of sports since Thomas Edison's invention, the light bulb, illuminated the very first night game at a seaside resort in Massachusetts.

One major contribution technology has made is in the way sporting events are delivered to the public. In the early days sporting events generally consisted of local teams playing one another. Fans were limited to following teams they were close enough to see in person. They could catch up on box scores in the newspaper and that was pretty much it.

Enter trains, planes, and automobiles and teams started traveling across the country and sometimes even the world to play each other. Radio made it possible for fans to listen in on games across the country and, when television came along, watching games became a national pastime.

Cut to the present and some households have televisions in almost every room—even the bathroom. Cable and satellite

FUN FACTOID

John McEnroe was the last Wimbledon finalist to use a wooden racquet in 1982.

"I know, but I had a better year than Hoover."

—BASEBALL GREAT BABE RUTH TO A REPORTER WHO OBJECTED THAT RUTH DEMANDED A HIGHER SALARY THAN THE PRESIDENT OF THE UNITED STATES, HERBERT HOOVER

delivery bring all kinds of sporting events into homes 24/7. All sports news channels like ESPN make keeping up with your favorite teams a piece of cake. And, if round-the-clock television coverage isn't enough, there's the Internet with an infinite amount of sports stats and live streaming of even more events. A few bucks and a high-speed Internet connection can get you a front row seat to watch your favorite team almost anytime. Thanks to technology, sports fans get unprecedented access to their favorite games while the pro sports industry rakes in even more moolah from all the new sports "products."

Wide World of Sports

Everyone knows that the iPod has revolutionized the way we listen to music and watch videos. It has also revolutionized the way that professional athletes prepare to play. Pro teams are staffed with video professionals who tape all their team's games. They can then edit special versions of each player's performance and upload it to their individual iPod.

Pitchers like Jason Jennings of the Colorado Rockies use their iPods to view footage of previous games. They analyze

New technology is even getting couch potatoes in the game!

their performance against batters that they're getting ready to face and see what worked and what didn't. Same thing with hitters. They can use their iPods to review footage of how they performed against a pitcher so they're better prepared next time.

Speaking of video, it has long been used to help athletes analyze their individual performances and help root out issues in mechanics. Computers paired with other high-tech devices take that concept even further by converting video images into 3-D. Baseball, basketball, tennis players, and golfers can analyze their swing, shot, or stroke in three dimensions from multiple angles and work with their coaches to figure out exactly where it is breaking down or how it can be enhanced.

The Doctor Is In

Sports medicine has become much more than treating and preventing injury in athletes. Athletes are now subjected to extensive testing that helps their coaching staff understand how their physiology will affect their performance. Testing reveals everything from an athlete's endurance capacity to their percentage of body fat and range of motion. With a scientific analysis of an athlete's strengths and weaknesses, a comprehensive program, including weight training, conditioning, and nutrition, can be developed to help the athlete maximize his or her performance.

Complex software programs are available to help athletes monitor their performance. They can track every detail related to their own nutrition, training regiment, and performance. Coaches, physicians, and other members of their training team can log in and help track their performance and spot any abnormalities.

High-tech Gear

Sports gear, a $55.7 billion business in 2005, is in a constant state of evolution. Basketball shoes have come a long way since Chuck Taylor All-Stars. The equipment pros use today has improved dramatically over what they used even a couple decades ago. Tennis shoes used to be canvas and rubber. Now Nike has introduced a line of shoes that includes a sensor that reports back to your iPod Nano and syncs your workout with voice-based feedback (that means it talks to you), including speed, distance, and calories burned—all set to your favorite workout music. Talk about high tech. Of course, Converse reissues the good 'ol All-Stars from

FUN FACTOID

The Nike swoosh logo, a globally recognized symbol, was purchased by Nike founder Phil Knight for $35 from an art school student.

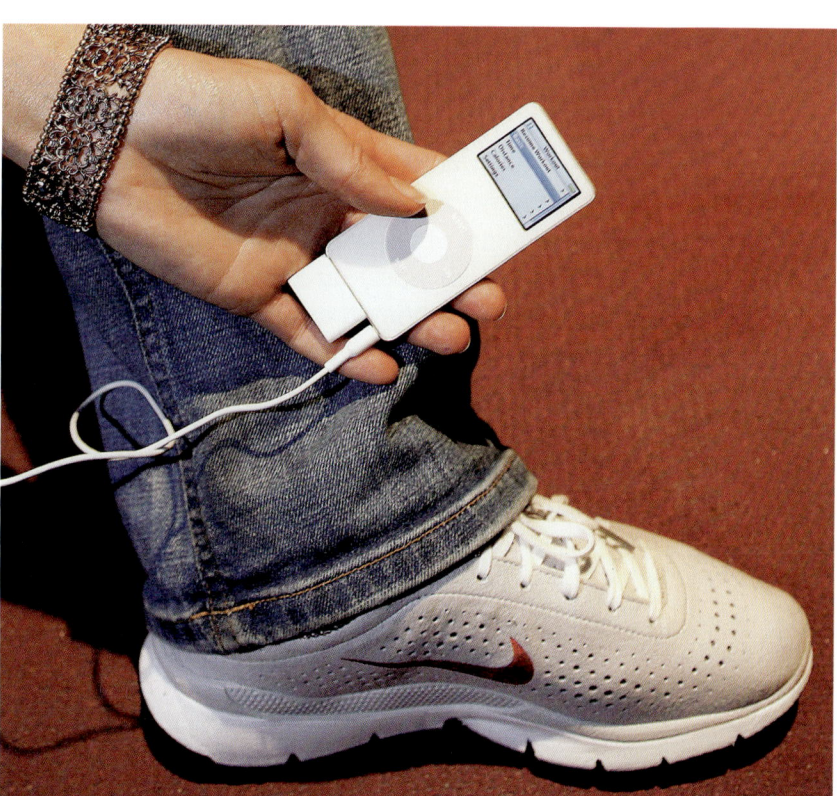

Sports gear goes high-tech.

Can You Take the Heat?

Professional athletes deal with the pressure of winning and losing every day. Your soccer team has just lost the state championship on penalty kicks. You respond by:

A Going into a tirade and blaming everyone from "the blind as a bat ref" to your no-talent teammate who missed her PK to your mom who forgot to pack your lucky socks.

B Refusing to shake hands with the victors and heading straight to the locker room to sulk.

C Bursting into tears on the sidelines and blaming yourself for the loss.

D Congratulating the winning team, waiting till you hit the locker room to show your disappointment, and objectively critiquing your own performance so you'll know what you can do better next time.

If you answered A, B, or C, you might want to think about whether you can handle the pressure to perform on a daily basis.

time to time for those non-techies who prefer to go retro with their feet.

Shoes aren't the only part of an athlete's wardrobe to go high-tech. Even the shirts on their backs are technological marvels that deal with a problem common to all athletes–sweat. Sweat is a fact of life for almost all athletes. The body has to sweat to regulate the body temperature, but if the sweat doesn't dry, it can wind up giving you chills. Today's athletic fabrics breathe better than ever and actually wick the moisture (sweat) from your body so it can evaporate. You probably have a Coolmax jersey or pair of shorts in your drawer at home. There's even a new fabric on the market that controls body odor. It claims you can wear it for several days without washing it and not scare away all your friends with your stench.

Can you imagine Roger Federer or Serena Williams on center court with a wooden tennis racquet? Even these tennis superstars would get blown off the court by the power generated by today's racquets made of synthetic composites. They have larger heads, are built for speed and power and barely resemble the racquets from the 1970s, which were predominately made of wood. Better technology and fitter athletes have changed the game. Andy Roddick has the fastest serve on record, clocking in at 155 miles per hour. Try being on the other end of that with a wood racquet!

Tennis great John McEnroe has been openly critical of today's power tennis, calling it boring, and advocates greater restrictions on racquet technology, but it's unlikely that we will see a return to wood racquets any time soon. Chuck Kriese, head coach at Clemson University, agrees. He said that. "The use of higher-tech rackets has made skill less important than the equipment itself; therefore, the sport is made somewhat less fun and interesting."

Golf clubs used to be crafted by blacksmiths out of heavy iron. Now, they are designed through the use of computer-aided design and are made of light-weight materials like titanium and graphite and some of them look pretty weird. In 1980 Dan Pohl was the PGA leader in driving distance with an average drive of 274.1 yards. In 2006 Bubba Watson was the leader with an average drive of 318.7 yards. That's a difference of 44.6 yards, a good chunk of which can be attributed to technological advances in his golf clubs.

Extreme Measures

It is impossible to address the trends in professional sports without at least touching on extreme sports. Extreme sports like skateboarding, inline skating, snowboarding, and BMX biking become less extreme and more mainstream every year. What makes a sport extreme? Speed, height, gravity, and at least a touch of danger. Athletes perform death-defying stunts that produce a huge adrenaline rush. ESPN's X Games have put extreme sports on the map and skateboarder Tony Hawk is the poster child. Hawk makes about $10 million a year thrilling crowds with his breathtaking stunts. And Shaun White, the Flying Tomato, became a household name with his gold-medal-winning snowboarding performance in the 2006 Winter Olympics.

Sports Meets Bad Science

Technological advances are not always a good thing. You can't pick up a newspaper or surf the net without reading about a professional athlete who has been implicated in a scandal involving performance-enhancing drugs. The achievements of athletes like

CHECK IT OUT

Elite athletes and their teams use sophisticated software to track everything that is going on with their body and their life. Go to http://www .freedownloadscenter. com and search "my training diary." You can use it to manage your training schedule and monitor your weight, diet, and performance just like a pro.

Who could have guessed that the invention of electricity would forever change the way sports are played?

Barry Bonds, Tyler Hamilton, and Mark McGwire will always be tainted because they have been linked with illegal performance-enhancing drugs.

Is it any wonder with the huge amount of money available to the best athletes that many resort to drugs in order to gain a competitive edge? Athletes who use anabolic steroids as a shortcut to strength and endurance do so at the risk of their overall mental and physical health, as their use comes with a lot of serious side effects.

There is an ongoing battle between technologies as the good guys work to develop ways to catch the cheaters and the cheaters work just as hard to find ways to avoid getting caught.

Quench That Thirst

Gatorade was invented by a team at the University of Florida's College of Medicine in 1965. The University of Florida Gators freshmen were used as guinea pigs to test the new concoction, which tasted horrible according to early reports. Following a scrimmage in which one team of freshmen drinking Gatorade came out in the second half and outplayed the other team, the Gators head coach, Ray Graves, requested some of the drink be provided for the varsity's game against LSU. After Florida came from behind to win in 102 degree heat, Gatorade was officially born and became a staple on Florida's sidelines as well as on sports fields across the world.

Of course, now there is a plethora of other sports drinks on the market, but none have quite the colorful history of Gatorade.

Dream Team

Thanks in equal parts to technology and to the fanatical devotion of millions of sports fans, fantasy sports have gown into a multibillion dollar industry. Fantasy sports involve groups of wannabe sports "owners" who build their personal version of a dream team by choosing players from a variety of real teams to play each position on their team. "Owners" compete with other "owners" based on the statistics generated by each of their players. For instance, you earn points when your quarterback makes a touchdown, your lineman makes a tackle, and so on.

According to the Fantasy Sports Trade Association, fantasy sports have grown to include as many as 19.4 million people aged 12 and up. They also estimate that 22 percent of adult males between the ages of 18 and 49 play fantasy games online. The Fantasy Sports Venture group of fantasy Web sites boast of drawing some five million unique visitors a month.

Don't kid yourself—these fantasy teams can get every bit as competitive as the real thing. Owners trade, cut, and sign players like real owners. And many fantasy sports leagues award prizes to winning teams.

CHAPTER 4

Training Camp

FUN FACTOID

WNBA players are required to graduate or complete four years of college eligibility before they can play.

Take a good bit of talent, mix in a healthy portion of self-discipline, add just the right amount of training, and a pinch of good luck, and you have all the ingredients it takes to become a pro athlete. Talent is definitely part of the mix. If you have two left feet and absolutely no hand/eye co-ordination, no amount of training or self-discipline is going to take you to the pros. So, be realistic. Do you have talent? If the answer is yes, the next question is, are you willing to put in the time?

Training for professional athletes begins early, usually before they even have a clue that they want to pursue a career in sports. It starts on the tee-ball fields, in soccer school, or on the peewee basketball court. It might start on a tennis court with mom gently pitching balls over the net or in the backyard playing catch or shooting hoops with Dad. If you are involved in recreational, club, or school sports, your training for a career as a professional athlete may have already begun.

Of course, not every sports pro starts as early as golf superstar Tiger Woods. Apparently, he was showing signs of becoming a golf protégé even as a toddler. He appeared on the *Mike Douglas Show* putting against comedian Bob Hope at

> **"If you train hard, you'll not only be hard, you'll be hard to beat."**
> **—HERSCHEL WALKER**

Little league today. Majors tomorrow?

the age of two. He also shot an impressive 48 over nine holes at age three.

Some young athletes enjoy playing a variety of sports before zeroing in on a favorite, but it is not uncommon for even very young athletes to specialize in one sport.

This was certianly the case for soccer superstar Mia Hamm, who said, "As soon as I made the national team at 15, I knew that

Who's Driving the Train?

Are you a certified sports nut? Do you live in total anticipation until your next sports event? Do you like your sport so much that you even look forward to practice sessions? Take this little quiz and find out if your motivation comes from you or an outside force or two.

	Me	Mom	Dad
Schedules my practice sessions.			
Reminds me to work on individual skills.			
Keeps up with my equipment.			
Motivates me to do my daily fitness.			
Keeps me on my training diet.			
Talks with my coach about important decisions.			

Tally up the check marks. If the majority of them fall in the Mom and Dad columns, it may be time to take some responsibility for your own sports career. Who are you doing this for? You or them?

I wanted to concentrate on soccer. It was my decision, not anyone else's. It was also when I began to understand what it took to work on my own. Until then, I didn't understand the game as much as I needed to."

Experts are divided on the wisdom of specialization at young ages, with some saying that injuries from overusing a particular part of the body is more common in one-sport athletes. Which is why it's a good idea for young athletes to have regular physical exams and to stay alert for any signs of recurring injury. As they say, "an ounce of prevention is worth a pound of cure."

Some athletic protégés pack their bags and spend their youth at sports academies like the IMG Academies in Bradenton, Florida. They attend a private school in the morning and train in their specific sport, like golf, tennis, or soccer, in the afternoon. Competitions fill up most weekends. Some prestigious alumni of the IMG training programs are Andre Agassi, Nomar Garciaparra, DaMarcus Beasley, and Maria Sharapova.

Most stay at home and work their way through the ranks of recreational and competitive sports teams. They start on the local recreation or YMCA fields and join increasingly more competitive teams as their skill and desire increase. At some point they may employ the services of an individual coach or trainer to help them work on the finer points of their game as well as their fitness and conditioning.

This will happen sooner for an athlete that participates in an individual sport like tennis or golf. They will learn their sport through group and private lessons and begin a relationship with a coach that can guide them through the ins and outs of their sport's tournament and ranking systems. Really good coaches will communicate with the young athlete's parents and help guide them in making appropriate decisions for their child's athletic career.

A Dream Come True

Sometimes parents get carried away and can push a kid toward a career in sports as a means to fulfill the parent's dream, not the kid's. This can be a problem for many reasons. If you find yourself in this situation, try some open communication with Mom and Dad before things get too out of hand. Make sure your dreams are *your* dreams.

Also, it is not unheard of for a coach to push an athlete too fast. The end result can be a great athlete who is burnt out and sick of playing because it has stopped being fun. Frequent communication between you, your parents, and your coach is a good idea to make sure you stay involved in the process and have some say in the direction your athletic career is headed.

Health and fitness is a lifelong concern for a professional athlete. Proper nutrition and hydration become important as soon as an athlete starts competing. A chili cheese dog, fries, and milkshake are not part of the pre-game meal of a champion.

And, in addition to the many hours of practicing the chosen sport, there are hours devoted to conditioning and strength training. There is great debate on what age is appropriate to begin strength training, so before you start working with weights, consult with an expert who will design a program especially for you and teach you how to do it properly. Your coach can hook you up with a professional trainer.

High school injuries sideline many dreams of pro careers.

Middle school and high school fields provide further training for future pros, although their importance varies depending on the sport. This experience is especially important for football, baseball, and basketball players. Less so for soccer, tennis players, and golfers. For them, playing high school sports is more a fun break from their more intense club or tournament teams.

The Next Step

What happens next depends on your sport and your life choices. Colleges and universities across the country are prime training ground for team athletes. And while many athletes cut their college careers short and opt to turn pro early, most benefit from at least a few years of college team experience.

Only the most talented baseball or basketball players jump straight to the pros and it's pretty much unheard of for a football player to skip college. Most players need the extra time to develop and for their bodies to mature. As previously mentioned, it's a good idea to take advantage of sports scholarships that provide free or discounted opportunities to go to college. The life expectancy of a sports career is short and, even if you make it to the big leagues, you'll eventually be looking for something else to do. So be prepared!

On Your Own

It's a totally different ball game for athletes that compete in individual sports like tennis or golf. Many tennis players, especially girls, skip college altogether and turn pro in their teens. Maria Sharapova joined the Nick Bollettieri Academy at age nine, signed her first contract with Nike and IMG at age 11, and played in her first pro tournament at age 15. Tennis star Andy Roddick skipped college, opting to turn pro instead. Tiger Woods attended Stanford University for three years before leaving early to turn pro.

Too much, too soon has caused some to flame out early due to injury or burnout. Tennis player Tracy Austin is an often-cited

---

Test Your Sports Vocab

POP QUIZ

See if you can fill in the blanks for the following sports lingo:

1 A two bagger is a _____.

 A Double play

 B Two base hit

 C Two point basket

2 An ace is a _____.

 A Another name for bogey

 B Really good lineman

 C Serve your opponent can't hit

3 A Hail Mary is a _____.

 A Long, desperate football pass

 B Long drive in golf

 C Long drive in a race car

4 A squeeze play is a _____.

 A Baseball play where the batter bunts in order to score a runner on third

 B Football play where two linemen sandwich the quarterback

 C A skateboarding move made famous by Tony Hawk

ANSWERS: 1-B, 2-C, 3-A, 4-A

example who bulldozed her way to tennis stardom at age 14 and was pretty much done by her 21st birthday due to the physical and emotional stresses of too much competition so soon.

For most athletes college is by far the best option. Those extra years give them the benefit of a free education and and a chance to explore what they really want to do with their lives. Take some advice from a tennis player who's been there—James Blake—who said, "For me, going to college was the best option. I wasn't physically or mentally ready to go pro when I was 17 years old and going into college. I was probably 140 pounds and would have gotten blown over by a stiff wind. So being out on tour, I would have gotten just eaten up. I don't think that would have helped my confidence, and I just wanted to go to college to improve on a bunch of things."

Athletes who go the college route must balance staying on top of their grades as well as their game. Some choose to major in sports management, sports medicine, or another sports-related subject, while others may opt for business, pre-law, or any other subject that interests them.

Eating healthy and staying fit are two ways to get ready for a career as an athlete.

Maintaining a good grade point average is just one of the very strict rules that govern college athletics. Messing around with the rules even by accident can knock you out of contention for a college scholarship and end your eligibility. Every athlete with scholarship ambitions should get well-acquainted with these rules. Check out all the recruiting and eligibility ins and outs at http://www.ncaa.org/wps/portal.

We all know that there is big money in sports, but it doesn't come to every athlete and it doesn't come without a price. Pro athletes sacrifice things that most of us take for granted, like our privacy and time with our family. Starting in middle school, or even earlier, elite athletes miss out on things that most of us consider normal, like going to birthday parties, hanging out with friends, going to the prom, or even

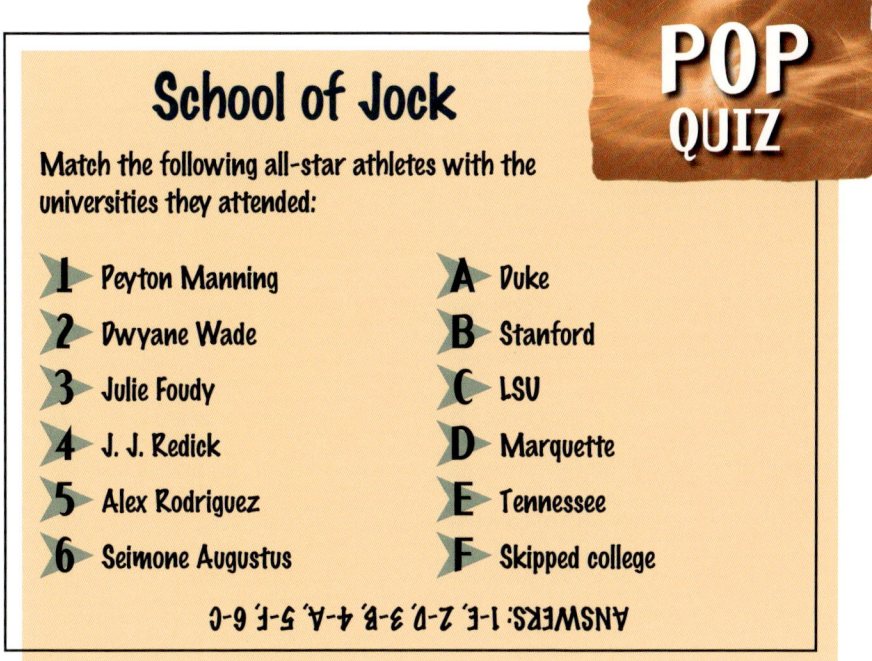

School of Jock

POP QUIZ

Match the following all-star athletes with the universities they attended:

1 ▶ Peyton Manning   A ▶ Duke

2 ▶ Dwyane Wade   B ▶ Stanford

3 ▶ Julie Foudy   C ▶ LSU

4 ▶ J. J. Redick   D ▶ Marquette

5 ▶ Alex Rodriguez   E ▶ Tennessee

6 ▶ Seimone Augustus   F ▶ Skipped college

ANSWERS: 1-E, 2-D, 3-B, 4-A, 5-F, 6-C

their own graduation because they feel like they can't pass up opportunities to be better at their sport.

The Next Step

Okay, couch potatoes, here's your cue to sit up and take notice. When you set out to become a professional athlete, it means that working out will be your total way of life. You don't sit behind a desk staring at a computer all week and then suit up on Sunday to tackle a 300 pound linesman (and live to tell about it, anyway). Professional athletes work out, day in and day out. More than once a day even. Running, jumping, pumping weights. It's all part of the job. So, bottom line, if you don't like pushing yourself to the limit, you won't like being a professional athlete.

Be real. Can you see yourself enjoying and excelling in such an active, physically demanding profession? Sure, you might not be quite there yet. The question is, are you willing to do what it takes to get there? Are you willing to get knocked down, pick yourself up, and do it all over again tomorrow? Your answer to that question will largely define whether or not you should even give this profession a second thought.

Teamwork

FUN FACTOID

So you eat, drink, sleep, and breathe sports, but after a gut check you realize that you might not have the talent, or the discipline, to be a professional athlete. Don't sweat it. While only a few thousand Americans earn their living as professional athletes, there are over 4.4 million working as part of the sports industry. Take a look at these jobs. They will keep you close to the action but won't require two-a-day training sessions or an unnatural obsession with your body mass index.

If you look hard enough, you'll find there's something for every talent and interest. Virtually anything you can do anywhere else in the business world, you can do in a sports-related way. Professional teams need accountants and marketing experts. Athletic facilities need people to manage all aspects of the the operation and news stations need sports journalists. All it takes is a little thinking outside the box to come up with a winning game plan.

So expand your horizons a little and see what you can find out about the many fascinating ways that people work to make sports happen. Try to imagine yourself doing each of the jobs you read about. Which sound most like a good fit with what you like to do and how you like to spend your time?

> "Whoever said, 'It's not whether you win or lose that counts,' probably lost."
>
> —MARTINA NAVRATILOVA, CHAMPION TENNIS PLAYER

Agent

Agents help athletes find jobs by promoting them to teams. They also negotiate all of their important business deals. An agent may "discover" an athlete while in high school or college and represent him during his entire career. They help athletes make extra money by negotiating endorsement deals like the $90 million shoe deal agent Aaron Goodwin negotiated with Nike for his client, LeBron James.

Athletic Director

If you love sports, are great with people and numbers, and are a stickler for the rules, you might want to consider a career as an athletic director. Athletic directors are in charge of all the sports programs at schools and universities. They hire and fire coaches, spend and raise money, and make sure that all the rules of their school's governing body are obeyed. Athletic directors, especially at the college level, spend years working their way up through the ranks of the athletic department, so it is not likely to be a job that you can snag right out of college.

Athletic Trainer

You know the guy or gal who comes out on the field to check on an injured player? It's probably the same guy or gal who taped all the ankles and knees prior to the game. That's the athletic trainer. Athletic trainers work as part of a team, which includes the coach and a physician, to help athletes avoid, evaluate, treat, and recover from injury. At the elite level they also design programs that include exercise and diet to enable athletes to maximize their performance.

NAME: C. Vivian Stringer

OFFICIAL TITLE: Coach

What do you do?

I am the head women's basketball coach at Rutgers University and there was a time when coaching basketball was about basketball. You coached and you worked with your players. Now you have to be a business person too. I have a lot of administrative responsibilities, including budgeting, marketing, and promotions. I manage a number of assistants. I have a press conference once a week and field media requests as they come up. I break down tapes of our opponents and analyze what they're doing and consider what we have to do defensively to counter it.

ON THE JOB

Recruiting is huge. On those days when I'm not coaching, I'm often flying across the country to see recruits. I spend probably 20 hours a week in the gym and three or four hours a day reviewing that day's practice tape and planning for the next day.

Of course, what I'm paid for, and the only part that people really see, is if I win or if I lose.

How did you get started?

I didn't plan to coach. I thought it was boring, but that's the only thing that I thought I could do that would allow me to stay in the game. I never thought that I would enjoy it the way that I have.

I took a job teaching at Cheney University. I went to see the president and asked him if I could coach the team. I had a vision and he could see my enthusiasm. I didn't get paid and all I asked was that they didn't schedule a class for me at 7:30 a.m. because we often got home really late.

I started getting paid to coach when I went to Iowa. I went there because my daughter was stricken with meningitis and Iowa had the largest teaching hospital in the world. I had other opportunities but Iowa stood out because they made sure that I wouldn't have to worry about my daughter's care. I spent 11 years there before joining Rutgers in 1995.

Most coaches won't be able to have the kind of longevity that I've been fortunate to enjoy because it has become so demanding. Still, I wouldn't trade it.

Coach

Coaches prepare athletes to compete. They work with players on an individual and team basis by teaching technique, tactics, and, everyone's favorite–conditioning. Coaches develop game plans based on what they know about their team's strengths and weaknesses as well as their opponents. Then they have to motivate their team to execute the plan. It is not uncommon for a professional athlete to take up coaching when they retire from the professional sports arena.

Facilities Manager

Most professional sports are played in multimillion dollar sports complexes. Every season millions of fans leave their mark (and their trash!) on these places. Someone has to make sure that the place is clean, safe, and full of the fan's favorite junk foods. This, along with attending to zillions of other details, is what a facilities manager does. Facilities managers tend to have a college background and experience in areas such as business administration, accounting, or marketing.

Personal Trainer

Personal trainers are high-energy fitness freaks that make their living motivating others to get and stay fit. They develop diet and exercise programs and teach their clients the proper use of exercise equipment. They may also teach group exercise classes such as aerobics or spinning.

Physical Education Teacher

Love 'em or hate 'em, physical education teachers provide a vital service to kids; they teach them to be healthy and fit, maybe even while having a little fun. While coaches may specialize in one sport, physical education teachers must be able to teach the basics of most sports. They also have to motivate kids who are athletically challenged and couch potatoes to be physically active.

Recreation Director

Another way to describe a recreation direction is director of fun. These sports-loving professionals run the parks and recreation programs that are found in cities and neighborhoods everywhere.

Some even find their way into positions aboard cruise ships or at fancy resorts. And, believe it or not, most of the successful ones actually have a college degree in recreation.

Scout

Scouts find new talent for their team by collecting information and statistics about exceptional athletes and attending sporting events to investigate prospects with potential. Much of their work is undercover since they don't want to let the competition know who they're after.

Sports Attorney

Wherever you find big money, you're bound to find attorneys making sure that their clients get their fair share of it. This is certainly true in the multibillion dollar sports industry. Sports attorneys must complete the same rigorous college training and state bar association tests as other lawyers, but they specialize in working with athletes, agents, sports leagues, and other types of sports-related organizations.

Sports Broadcaster

Are you a sports whiz able to dazzle your friends with the massive amount of sports information at the tip of your tongue? Have you never met a camera that you didn't like? Then, by all means, explore a career as a sports broadcaster. Sports broadcasters report on sports on the radio and TV. Some sports broadcasters, like Dan Patrick and Scott Van Pelt from ESPN's *Sportscenter*, talk about sports in general while others provide play-by-play game commentary. This is another popular second career for many professional athletes.

Sports Information Director

The sports information director's (SID) job is to fill arena seats by generating interest in their team through the media. They write game reports and distribute them to interested media outlets. They arrange interviews with coaches and players. They keep track of team and player statistics and prepare game programs and other publications that make the team look good in print.

NAME: **Mary Carillo**

OFFICIAL TITLE: **Sports Broadcaster**

What do you do?

I do different things for the four different networks I work for. For ESPN, I do their tennis coverage. For HBO, I'm on *Real Sports with Bryant Gumbel* and *Inside the NFL*. For CBS, I cover the U.S. Open Tennis Championships. For NBC, I cover the French Open, Wimbledon and the Olympics.

My work for HBO is totally different. If I'm working on a profile piece, it's pretty straight up; it doesn't take much time but if you're really trying to craft a story it could take you anywhere and it could take a long time.

One day on the job is different from any other. The tennis is the only part of my job where I know where I'm going to be and I know what it's going to be. I'm fluent in that sport. I'm not fluent in all these other sports and there are so many different athletes to learn about.

How did you get started?

I had been playing professional tennis and I was known as a bit of a lively interview. Win or lose, I always had something to say after a match. My last tournament was Wimbledon in 1980 and I didn't know what I was going to do. I had called a match at Madison Square Garden for free and a producer who had just been assigned to produce women's tennis happened to hear it and he called me with an offer. As luck would have it, I was madly available. It started that way, and for a couple of years all I did was a couple of women's events.

As my career progressed, whenever I was asked if I could do something new, like an idiot I always said, yes. There was nothing terribly planned about all this except that my first instinct was always to say, "Oh, absolutely I can do that! Absolutely! How hard can it be?" And then if I stink, they'll fire me. I wasn't trying to break the glass ceiling or anything, I just kept saying, yes. And more than yes—Absolutely! I just assumed that the work was something I could enjoy and do. And if I was going to get found out, then I was willing to go with that too. One of these days someone's going to tap me on the shoulder and tell me I've gone too far, and I will leave quietly.

ON THE JOB

NAME: John Todd

OFFICIAL TITLE: Sports Photographer

What do you do?

I take assignments from publications like *Sports Illustrated, ESPN, the Magazine, Soccer America, Fair Game Magazine, 90:00 Minutes Magazine*, or the U.S. Soccer Federation and cover specific games that are requested. I go to the games, shoot them and within an hour, process all the digital files and upload those to our database, where our clients come to browse and download images for their publications.

I spend about four hours a day on administrative work. There is so much business involved in photography now. It's not just about getting the photo. I spend maybe 30 percent of my time out in the field making images. About 25 percent of my job is going out and looking for new clients.

ON THE JOB

How did you get started?

I started photography in the seventh grade, processing black and white images in the lab and I just fell in love with the process. I took photo classes in high school, but I really didn't do sports photography because I was playing sports.

When I went to college, I worked for my college newspaper and found that I enjoyed shooting sports. It was fun being on the sidelines and as close to the action as possible.

I was a history major in college and thought about being an attorney but the photography side was so exciting. I did an internship when I graduated and then worked for a small newspaper in Connecticut for three years. I moved back to the San Francisco Bay area in the 90s and started freelancing. After the 1994 World Cup, they announced that they were going to have a Major League Soccer team in San Jose and I bugged the sports information director for about a year until he finally gave me a chance to come shoot for them. They hired me and I started at the first game and worked for the San Jose Earthquakes for 10 years until they moved to Houston. I also freelanced for clients like the Associated Press and Stanford University. I was the director of photography for a women's sports magazine called *Real Sports Magazine* and chief photographer for the American Basketball League, which preceded the WNBA. In 2002 I took over International Sports Images.

Sports Event Manager

There are a million details that go into making any sporting event work. Just for starters, teams have to be scheduled to play, tickets have to be printed and sold, and the event has to be promoted to the community so people will know to come. The sports event manager has a hand in attending to all the details that go into pulling off successful sporting events.

Sports Photographer

You've seen them crowding the sidelines at every major sports event. You might have even spotted one covering your club or school match. Except for athletes, no one gets closer to the action than a sports photographer. Sports photographers capture images of sporting events for use in newspapers, magazines, and Web sites, and they usually have the best seat in the house.

Sports Psychologist

As sports have become increasingly competitive, athletes seek to get even the slightest edge; that includes making sure their mental game is on. Sports psychologists teach athletes techniques like visualization and imagery to help them mentally prepare to compete at their best. They also work with teams to build unity through team building exercises.

Umpire or Referee

We all love to hate the men in stripes. It's their job to make sure that everyone plays by the rules, and sometimes the players, coaches, and fans don't like their decisions. Just like athletes, umpires and refs learn their craft on the Little League, recreation, and school fields. Over time, a select few climb all the way to the top and make a living calling games at the highest level like the World Cup, the World Series, or the Super Bowl.

CHAPTER 6

Kids Ask, Athletes Answer

FUN FACTOID

The average salary for professional athletes is $48,310. Is that considered good money? Find out how it compares to other professionals such as doctors, lawyers, and teachers at the U.S. Department of Labor's kid's Web site at http://www.bls.gov/k12/index.htm.

How did we find out what kids really wanted to know about being a professional athlete? We asked them! We asked students at Simon Baruch Middle School in New York City and Greenbrier Middle School in Evans, Georgia, what they would ask a professional athlete about their job if they had the chance. Real-life professional athletes Cat Reddick Whitehill, James Blake, and Stephen Drew were kind enough to provide the answers.

Cat, James, and Stephen all play sports for a living. Cat is a professional soccer player and she competes with the U.S. Women's National Team. She won a gold medal in the 2004 Olympic games in Athens, Greece, and is preparing to compete in the 2007 FIFA Women's World Cup. James is a professional tennis player and is currently ranked number four in the world. Stephen is a shortstop for the Arizona Diamondbacks. He completed his first season as a pro in 2006 after being heavily recruited out of Florida State University.

When you did you decide that you wanted to become a professional athlete?

—Lucia Z., age 13

"...what **better job** is there out there than to be able to **play** the sport that you **love.**"

—CAT REDDICK WHITEHILL

James Blake

Cat: Once I realized that I actually could be a professional athlete. I always wanted to play but I didn't think that I would actually be able to do it because I was a woman and a soccer player and there weren't that many opportunities. When I was in college, the WUSA started, and right then I wanted to be a professional athlete because what better job is there out there than to be able to play the sport that you love.

Stephen: When I was probably about 12.

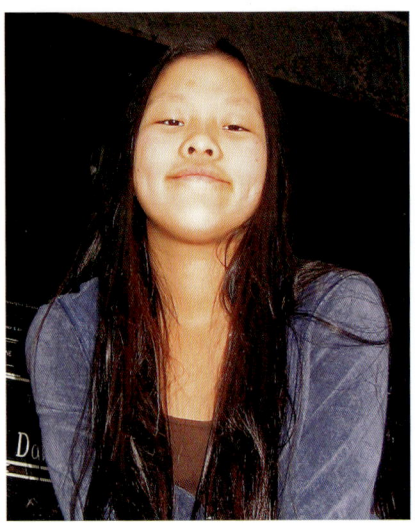

Lucia Z.

James: I decided I wanted to be a professional athlete after I had success at the college level and when I realized that to keep improving I needed to be pushed more and more by better players every day.

If you could go back in time would you still be doing what you are doing?

—Tian C., age 12

Cat: Absolutely. I would rather be a professional soccer player than anything else I could be doing. It is definitely an honor to be representing the United States and it's a lot of fun. I get to practice and work out every day and I'm getting paid to do it. It's fun to have little girls look up to you and have the responsibility of being a role model. I look at it sometimes and I'm like, "Wow, I am so fortunate to have such an incredible opportunity."

Stephen: Yes, I could not be happier.

James: If I could go back in time, I would definitely still be doing what I do now. I love playing tennis and wouldn't want to be doing anything else right now.

How old were you when you first played your sport and how did you do?

—Lindiana T., age 11 and Michael T., age 13

Cat: I started playing soccer when I was five years old and I played with boys and girls at that time. I think I did well. My mom has a video of me and I put my hand up to show my mom that I had just scored my fifth goal. I think that kind of shows that I did alright.

Stephen: I played T-ball when I was five years old.

James: I first starting playing tennis when I was about five years old and I started taking lessons when I was 11. I wasn't too good when I started, but I had a lot of fun.

Have you ever gotten stopped on the street because someone freaked out when they realized who you were and got really excited?

— Emily L., age 13

Cat: I have, and being a female soccer player, you don't get that as often as some other professional athletes but it has happened and it's a really cool experience because you don't think people will recognize you in street clothes.

Stephen: No, not yet.

James: I have been stopped on the street quite a few times by people who recognize me. I always am surprised by it because it is tough to adjust to people knowing who you are.

Do you play because you love the sport or because you can make a lot of money?

—Kori W., age 14

Cat: I play because I love the sport. Money has nothing to do with the reason why I'm playing soccer, it's just an added perk. Soccer is so much fun and it's a great way to meet different people and make great friends and get exercise every day. The game of soccer is so much fun. I would play without the money.

Stephen: I play because I love baseball, but it is my job and I have to provide for my family.

James: I play the sport because I love it. I have been playing tennis for 20 years, and only getting paid for it for about six. I plan on playing tennis long after I can get paid for playing.

How much do you have to practice every day?

—Tony B., age 13

Cat: With the National Team, I would say that we practice with the ball about two hours every day and then we lift weights for about an hour after that. It's really only about three hours, which is actually nice. The way that we practice is so intense, you can really only take about two hours or your body wouldn't be able to take it anymore.

Stephen: I practice when I need to.

James: I practice for different amounts of time; it depends how close to a tournament it is. Most days I practice for about two hours and then work out after that.

What are some things you've had to give up to be a professional athlete?

–Lindsay Y., age 13

Cat: Some of the things that I've had to give up were like being a normal college student. Missing things like the homecoming dance or the prom. Sometimes I've had to miss out on my birthday or having Thanksgiving with my family.

Stephen: I am away from home all the time so I miss my family and friends among other things.

James: I had to give up some social activities during my youth to be a professional athlete. There were always things that my friends would do that I had to miss because of tennis. I also had to quit playing other sports that I enjoyed to focus on being the best tennis player I could be.

What is the hardest part of being an athlete?

– Kelly D., age 13

Cat: The hardest part is missing out and being away from your friends and family. Being away from my husband, being away from my mom and dad and my sister and my best friend is hard. Some of our vacations have become my soccer games, so we've had some great experiences too.

Stephen: The hardest part about being a professional athlete is trying to be consistent all the time.

James: The hardest part of being a professional athlete is traveling and not getting to see your friends and family as much as you would like.

What is the best aspect of playing professional sports?

—David B., age 13

Cat: Just that; playing a sport for a living. Soccer is something that I've loved since I was five and getting to play that every day is awesome. And the way our schedule works, I was just with the team in Korea for two weeks and so we have the next two weeks off so I can go anywhere I want, so I get to do some fun stuff. I get to travel all around the world. There are so many more perks than there are negatives.

Cat Reddick Whitehill

Stephen: I think for me it gives me a different viewpoint on life.

James: The best part of being a professional athlete is getting to do what you love every day. I get to work outdoors in a T-shirt and shorts and I love it.

What were your goals as an athlete when you were in middle school?

—Forrest B., age 13

Cat: When I was in middle school, my main goal was to make the regional ODP (Olympic Development Program) team. That was because one of my friends had made it and I wanted to know what that was like. Being from Alabama, I don't think I even realized that there was anything beyond regional. When they asked me to be on the U-16 National Team, I was kind of confused.

53

Stephen: I don't think I really had goals when I was in middle school. I just wanted to play the game.

James: My goals as an athlete have always been the same and that is to keep improving. So, in middle school I just wanted to get better to play on my high school team, and then the end goal keeps changing as you improve.

Is it really hard to deal with the pressure of winning?

–Kaitlin C., age 14

Cat: No, I love the pressure of winning. I think that's what makes it more fun. You have the pressure of winning and losing. You have to learn to be a good winner and a good loser, but when you remember the feeling of winning it's totally worth it.

Stephen: Sometimes it can be difficult.

James: I deal with the pressure by just remembering that it is always just a game. We play for fun and do our best, but it is still just a game that we are playing and I will always have friends and family no matter what the result of a tennis match is.

Tian C.

Do you have any time at all just to have fun?

–Rita P., age 14

Cat: Absolutely. During the times when we're off, we definitely have fun. Every chance I get, I hang out with my husband and my friends and family. To me, that's a lot of fun because when you miss out on that, you realize how important it is. Even when the team is on the road, we have a lot of fun together.

Stephen: In the off-season I get to hunt and fish.

James I have time to have just fun, but not as much as I would like. I love to play golf and poker when I do have time off.

Do you ever miss your family and friends when you are on the road?

–Tian C., age 13

> **Cat**: I miss my friends and family a lot. They are a very special part of me. They've made me the person that I am and not being there every day with them is really hard for me.
>
> **Stephen**: Yes, I miss my family and friends a lot when I am on the road but it helps when I can talk with them on the phone or chat on iChat.
>
> **James:** I miss my family and friends all the time when I am on the road. I get to stay in touch pretty well by email and the phone with all of them, but it is still great to see them when I come home.

What advice would you give a middle school student who was thinking about a career as a professional athlete?

–Austin B., age 12

> **Cat:** Just keep playing and keep having fun. I was just a little girl from Alabama and no one ever thought that I could do it. With the support of your family and the desire to do it, if you keep practicing, stay focused, and still have fun, I think there's a whole lot more that you can do that you never knew you could.

CHAPTER 7

Virtual Apprentice

ATHLETE FOR A DAY

Being a professional athlete is all about talent, hard work, and discipline. Here is a day's worth of activities to see if you're made of the right stuff. Try it on your own or talk a teacher into making it into a class project.

8:00 Eat a healthy breakfast. Healthy means light on the refined sugar and fat, so forget about the donuts, Coco Puffs, and bacon. Some fresh fruit, a protein smoothie, and a whole wheat bagel with peanut butter would be more in the ballpark.

9:00 Go for a brisk run, swim, or bike ride. Daily aerobic exercise is part of a healthy lifestyle for everyone, but it is a critical component for maintaining the fitness you will need to enjoy a long athletic career. Get used to it. It will be a part of your daily routine for a long time.

10:00 Take your fitness a step closer to a professional level by creating a weekly schedule that blends weight training, aerobic workouts, and skill training in your sport of choice. Make a chart listing your daily schedule. For inspiration go online to http://verbnow.com.

11:00 Schedule a meeting with your coach. Prepare ahead of time to discuss your upcoming match and practice schedule. Work up the nerve to talk about your dreams of becoming a professional athlete. Ask for an honest assessment of where you're at athletically and discuss your strengths and weaknesses. You want honesty, so be ready to hear the good, the bad, and the ugly. Ask for specific suggestions of things you need to do to take it to the next level and take notes so that you can add them to your training schedule.

12:00 Time for a healthy lunch. Make it balanced and lay off the sweets and soft drinks.

1:00 Time to do some research about your favorite college sports team. Go online to find out all you can about the college, the team, its players, and the team's record. Pretend you are the team's scout and it's your job to recruit promising new players. Use the information you just discovered to create a brochure you could use to introduce the program to high school coaches and their star players.

2:00 Hit the court, it's practice time. Practice like you've never practiced before. Give every drill 110 percent. Lead the pack through conditioning and pay attention to your coach like he actually knows what he's talking about. Leave it all out on the court and practice like your livelihood depends on it because if your dream comes true, it will.

3:00 Use this time to work on an individual area of your game that's been giving you trouble. Maybe you've been double faulting a lot and need to work on your second serve. Perhaps you've had trouble finishing shots in game situations. Grab a buddy who will play goalie and just focus on your shot. Or, maybe you've been running out of gas near the end of games and just need to suck it up and invest some more time in your conditioning. Your coach might have a heart attack if he sees you running extra sprints after practice but it will be worth it to improve your game. Take responsibility to be the best you can be.

4:00 Whether they like it or not, professional athletes are role models. The great ones use their name, resources, and time to help worthy causes. Find a volunteer opportunity and begin the habit of giving back. It shouldn't be too hard to find a worthwhile way to spend an hour. Here are some ideas to get the juices flowing: tutor a student, volunteer to help coach a young rec team, or give an hour to a soup kitchen. Even if you decide that sports are not for you, it will be a good thing to incorporate into your schedule.

5:00 Watch a game. One way good athletes get better is by watching others play their game at the highest levels. Keep a notebook handy and spend some time analyzing the game. Try and figure out what makes the great players stand out. What makes them special? Are they qualities that you have or can incorporate into your game?

Virtual Apprentice
PROFESSIONAL ATHLETE: FIELD REPORT

If this is your book, use the space below to jot down a few notes about your Virtual Apprentice experience (or use a blank sheet of paper if this book doesn't belong to you). What did you do? What did you learn? Which activities did you enjoy the most? Don't be stingy with the details!

8:00 BREAKFAST: _____

_____

9:00 WORK OUT: _____

_____

_____

_____

10:00 TRAINING SCHEDULE: _____

_____

_____

_____

11:00 COACH MEETING: _____

_____

_____

_____

_____

_____

12:00 LUNCH: _____

_____

1:00 RESEARCH TEAMS: _____

_____

_____

_____

2:00 PRACTICE TIME: _____

_____

_____

_____

_____

_____

3:00 FOCUS ON TROUBLE SPOTS: _____

_____

_____

_____

_____

_____

4:00 ROLE MODEL: _____

_____

_____

_____

_____

_____

5:00 WATCH A GAME: _____

_____

_____

Count Me In (or Out)

ON THE SIDELINES OR IN THE GAME?

Sports are your life. You've dreamed about playing in the big leagues since you were a kid. You think you might have what it takes, but how can you be sure? These questions will help you think it through. Answer them on a separate piece of paper and look back at them after you sign your first pro contract.

When the game is on the line, I

❑ fade into the background because I'm afraid to fail.

❑ want the ball! I love having the game in my hands.

Playing in front of a crowd

❑ gives me a rush!

❑ makes me nervous as heck!

What makes me special as an athlete is _____

_____

_____

_____

_____

_____

The idea of getting up every morning and eating a healthy breakfast and making myself go for a run is

❑ never going to happen.

❑ just fine with me.

The idea of becoming a professional athlete

❑   makes total sense because: _____

_____

_____

_____

❑   makes NO sense because: _____

_____

_____

_____

_____

As for a career as a pro athlete

❑   Alert the media! Here's what I'm going to do to make it happen:

_____

_____

_____

_____

❑   I love sports but what I really want to do is:

_____

_____

_____

_____

_____

APPENDIX

More Resources for Young Athletes

BOOKS

Fleck, Steven J. *Strength Training for Young Athletes*. Champaign, Ill.: Human Kinetics, 2005.

Heitzmann, William Ray. *Careers for Sports Nuts & Other Athletic Types*. New York: McGraw-Hill, 2004.

Litt, Ann. *Fuel for Young Athletes: Essential Foods and Fluids for Future Champions*. Champaign, Ill.: Human Kinetics, 2005.

Reeves, Diane Lindsey and Lindsey Clasen. *Career Ideas for Kids Who Like Sports*. New York: Facts On File, 2007.

Smith, David Allen. *From the Prom to the Pros: The Athlete's, Parent's and Coach's Guide*. Santa Ana, Calif.: Seven Locks Press, 2000.

PROFESSIONAL ASSOCIATIONS

Major League Baseball Players Association
12 East 49th Street, 24th Floor
New York, New York 10017
http://mlbplayers.mlb.com/NASApp/mlb/pa/index.jsp

National Basketball Players Association
310 Lenox Avenue
New York, New York 10027
http://www.nbpa.com

Women's National Basketball Players Association
310 Lenox Avenue
New York, New York 10027
http://www.wnbpa.com/index.php

National Football League Players Association
2021 L Street, NW, Suite 600
Washington, D.C. 20036
http://www.nflpa.org/main/default.aspx

National Hockey League Players' Association
20 Bay Street, Suite 1700
Toronto, Ontario M5J 2N8
http://www.nhlpa.com/index.asp

U.S. National Soccer Team Players Association
725 Twelfth Street, NW
Washington, D.C. 20005
http://www.ussoccerplayers.com

Association of Tennis Professionals
201 ATP Tour Boulevard
Ponte Vedra Beach, Florida 32082
http://www.atptennis.com/1/en/home

Women's Tennis Association
One Progress Plaza, Suite 1500
St. Petersburg, Florida 33701
http://www.sonyericssonwtatour.com

WEB SITES

Kidzworld – Kid and Teen Sports Zone
http://www.kidzworld.com/site/the_zone.htm

The Women's Sports Foundation – Know Your Rights
http://www.womenssportsfoundation.org

INDEX